SPIRALING SPHERES

By

J.J. BHATT

ISBN:

9798841399162

Title:

Spiraling Spheres

Author:

J.J. Bhatt

Published and Distributed by Amazon and
Kindle worldwide.

This book is manufactured in the Unites States of America.

Recent Books by J.J. Bhatt

(Available from Amazon)

HUMAN ENDEAVOR: *Essence & Mission/ A Call for Global Awakening, (*2011)

ROLLING SPIRITS: *Being Becoming /*A Trilogy, (2012)

ODYSSEY OF THE DAMNED: *A Revolving Destiny,* (2013).

PARISHRAM: *Journey of the Human Spirits*, (2014).

TRIUMPH OF THE BOLD: *A Poetic Reality*, (2015).

THEATER OF WISDOM, (*2016).*

MAGNIFICENT QUEST: *Life, Death & Eternity,* (2016).

ESSENCE OF INDIA: *A Comprehensive Perspective,* (2016).

ESSENCE OF CHINA: *Challenges & Possibilities*, (2016).

BEING & MORAL PERSUASION: *A Bolt of Inspiration*, (2017).

REFELCTIONS, RECOLLECTIONS & EXPRESSIONS, (2018).

ONE, TWO, THREE... ETERNITY: *A Poetic Odyssey, (*2018).

INDIA: *Journey of Enlightenment*, (2019a).

SPINNING MIND, SPINNING TIME: *C'est la vie*, (2019b).Book 1.

MEDITATION ON HOLY TRINITY, *(2019c), Book 2.*

ENLIGHTENMENT: *Fiat lux*, (2019d), Book 3.

BEING IN THE CONTEXTUAL ORBIT: *Rhythm, Melody & Meaning, (*2019e).

QUINTESSENCE: *Thought & Action,* (2019f).

THE WILL TO ASCENT: *Power of Boldness & Genius,* (2019g).

RIDE ON A SPINNING WHEEL: *Existence Introspected, (*2020a).

A FLASH OF LIGHT: *Splendors, Perplexities & Riddles,* (2020b).

ON A ZIG ZAG TRAIL: *The Flow of Life*, (2020c).

UNBOUNDED: *An Inner Sense of Destiny* (2020d).

REVERBERATIONS: The *Cosmic Pulse,* (2020e).

LIGHT & DARK: *Dialogue and Meaning,* (2021a).

ROLLING REALITY: *Being in flux, (2021b).*

FORMAL SPLENDOR: *The Inner Rigor,* (2021c).

TEMPORAL TO ETERNAL: *Unknown Expedition,* (2021d).

TRAILBLAZERS: *Spears of Courage*, (2021e).

TRIALS & ERRORS: *A Path to Human Understanding*, (2021f).

MEASURE OF HUMAN EXPERIENCE: *Brief Notes,* (2021g).

LIFE: *An Ellipsis (2022a).*

VALIDATION: *The Inner Realm of Essence* (2022b).

LET'S ROLL: *Brave Heart,* (2022c).

BEING BECOMING (2022d).

INVINCIBLE (2022e).

Also: THE CODE: *DESTINY* (2022f); LIFE DIMYSTIFIED (2022g); ESSENTIAL HUMANITY (2022h); MORAL ADVENTURE (2022i); SPIRALING SPHERES (2022h).

4

Preface

SPIRALING SPHERES is an embodiment of the on-going challenges of our time: the general societal insecurity stemming from asymmetric wealth distributions, fear of the climate change, living in the world of fake news, cyber hackings and so on. Against such a constant destructive trend seem humans are heading toward a doomsday scenario. It is therefore essential; we regain our collective moral and rational endeavor; even common-sense and be the daring agents of positive change in the world.

SPIRALING SPHERES however reminds, we must not drop our guards as we are essentially running out of time; taking right action today is a must. Our collective escape is to wake-up first from all the ancient differences and be unified in our mission and immediately address the contemporary issues as mentioned, before it is too late.

SPIRALING SPHERES in essence holds that humanity does not need criticism but the encouragement to move on for the good of the whole. In other words, we must meet our planetary as well as societal responsibilities as grown-ups; leaving a better world for our children and theirs to live well.

J.J. Bhatt

Contents

9

The
Riddle

There is
A giant
Mirror without
An image

When I
Stare a bit,
I see
My image in it
And, it vanishes
Quickly

Oh yes,
It's a reality
Without essence
Yet it sparks and
Mercurially disappears
From my thought only

What a
Mysterious
Image of "I"
Holding my truth
And still there is
Nothing, but the
Riddle in the mind
Only!

Humanity
Matters

**Humanity is
Here to evolve
Toward good**

**There is never
In-between either
Good or evil,**

**Only
The old habits to
Be refined and be
The hero of your
This only chance,
Simply**

**Let humanity
Arise with its
Will and let
All shall
Be free from the
Guilt and grief**

**Humanity
Born
To be the spark
Of hope ever
Let it evolve
In harmony with
All That Is Good...**

The Glow

We are the
Glow in the
Darkness

We're the
Clarity to be
In this chaotic
Existence

Let us
Not be afraid to
Walk through the
Tunnel of anxiety
And fear

In the
End we shall
Be the light as
We shall
Regain our original
Meaning to be...

Gist

Let Truth
Be the
Conceptual
Justification to
Be humans

In its
Absence,
We may
Dwell into the
Cave forever

We're
The intelligent
Beings demanding
A necessity to have
An evolving reality
With a meaning

In its
Absence,
We may not bring
The closure,
"Who we're and what
We can become."

Invitation

Folks
Come and let us
Discover our
Collective worth
In this world of
Beauty and
Truth

Let us
Continue to be
The moral force
To test our worth

Come let us
Take a stand and
Act with the sincerity
Of our collective
Purpose

No point in
Thinking too long
No point in
Waiting too long
For the time is
Sneakily
Slipping away

Come and let us
Together give a
Meaning to
Our noble births...

Turning
Point

Why not
Ask, "What
Variable is missing
From the human
Equation"

Why not
Ask for clarity,
"What is a being,
Born in human
Form"

And, why
His truth is
Buried beneath
False narratives
And pseudo tribal
Claims for a long

Time to
Leave the myopic
Cage and time to
Be free to evolve
Toward a higher
Inspiring experience...

Odyssey

Alas
We're missing
The great opp to
Know the depth of
Inner being, our
Possibilities and the
Total reality in this
Misguided trend

If we're
Intelligent minds
With infinite
Curiosity and
Creativity,

Why not then
The odyssey of
Every being must
Begin

That is the
Way to enjoy
Greater freedom,
Harmony and to gain
A deep moral strength...

The
Force

Let us
Awake and
Face the challenges
That 've been on the
Deck for sometime

Is it not
Time to be the
Enlightened agents of
Positive change

Why not
Roll-up the sleeves
And be the willing
Force of our time

Let us
Adapt to the new
Realities of our
Collective destiny

Let us
Be in one unified
Mediation mode to
Discover, "Who we
Really are at the core."

Diary

In this
Little diary,
Where
I've saved a
Few thoughts and
Memories to know
The Self better than
Before

It's my
Personal identity
It's my alter-ego
It's my shadow and
It's my introspection
Too

Oh this
Petite few pages
Reflecting stream of
My silent consciousness
Mirroring, "Who am I"

Of course,
This little diary is
A treasure of my time
Yet, am the temporary
Owner of it while the
Journey's on...

Spiral,
Indeed

Dear Heart,
We're in love, but
We're lost in many
Doubts and debates

And that is
Where we've been
For a very long

You can
Punch me
Today, but don't
Forget to remember
Me tomorrow

I say it again,
"You can criticize
Me today, but
You'll know
Me tomorrow"

In such
Uncertainties of
Love, hope and
Life, I ask you to
Remember well,
"Sadly, we've
Forgotten,
How to be steady
In love with full trust..."

Indefatigable

Essence and
Existence seems
Tied-up with the
Deeper grasp of
Our collective worth

It's been
A spiraling sphere
Of love, luck and life
To roll off and on;
Wondering never
Stops

Human
Always the
Center of his
Intention and
Imperfection

And still
Retaining
Audacity to keep
The journey going

Let him
Keep walking and
Walking...walking to
His final truth...

Reality
As Is

We're the
Consequential
Beings albeit
The juggernaut
Force of change

We're
The essence
And we're the
Rhythm, melody
And meaning of
This existence

At times,
We're the
Tragedy of our
Own makings but
We persevere
Through thick and
Thins

That is the
Story, that is the
Glory and reality
Where we're the
Continuum into this
Mighty wild Sea...

The
Thrust

Know
We're rational
Beings that are
The illumined gifts
To have arrived on
The scene

We're
Challenged
To scan through
The thick layers of
Perceptions,
Assumptions and
The distortion of
All kinds and

Derive at
Some definite
Grasp of the Self
And the world around
For sure
That is our
Common thread
Of the whole

Also
Remember well,
To question, "Why there is
So much imperfection to
Be resolved?"

Life

Life
Stubbornly
Keeps
Coming back
Like a
Hydra headed
Queen; time after
Time

Life
What a colorful
Garden of dreams
And to be free, but
Be ready to tackle
Its thorns too

Life
What a chance
To grasp the deep
Meaning of it all and
Be aware it's a burning
Patch of trail as well

Life
What a great
Responsibility to
Keep it safe and well
And still be calm
And alert always...

The
Process

Through
Constructive
Criticisms and
Debates,
There is a
Chance to resolve
A given issue at hand

In doing
So, better
Understanding
And right action
Is a must

Only then we
Free ourselves
Bit by bit from the
Tight grips of the
Seven sin

In doing
So, we shall roll
Inch by inch
To the Temple of
Our
Collective Truth...

Echoes

In the
Silent night of
The deep winter
I hear echoes

From
The inner
Sanctum of the
Awakened humanity:

Let us bury
This world of
Jingoism, tribalism
And the insanity of
Violence's and wars

Time to
Drop yesterdays
Old habits of deaths
And destructions

Time to
Open-up our
Hearts and minds
To strengthen

One mighty
United Global Spirit
In the name of our
Children's sake...

What is Love!

What do we
Know of love,
If at all

Is it a
Fantasy or
Reality or what

Lovers
On trial in
Most short term
Relationship

Love
Turning into truth
After it endures for
A very long

That is
Why when lovers
Celebrate their
25th, 50th or ever longer;
We salute 'em with
Full-respect...

The
Journey

Human
Dimension is
The main issue
Of contention at
All time

For human
Is the main drive
To link his soul with
The totality of all
That is; even unknown
To the conscious mind

Questioning
His very essence
And existence is
The first spark of
His journey to be
Welcomed

And let the
Eternal quest
Never ends but the
Conceptual map of his
Reality keeps vividly
Clarifying with time...

Big
Picture

It all
Begins with
A right
Understanding and
In turn pointing,
"In what direction
To flow"

And the
Right flow is the
Consciousness;
Leading
To the magnifique
Realm of logic and
Moral thought

Consequently,
We're the
Enlightened
Spirits to reckon,

"Where
We come from,
Where
We're today and
Where
We ought to be
Going from this
Moment on..."

Sweet
Gal

Hey
Gal, keep
The sweet smile
Going forever

Hey
Gal, are you
Playing games
With me or what

Hey
Sweetie,
Don't you care
To call me, tonight

Remember,
Once
We're lovers
And now you act
As if we never met
Before

Hey
Janus gal,
What happened
To your pure love!
I am
Still, waiting for
Your sweet answer...

Action,
Only

There is
Time to make
It all again

Yes, there is
A way to be free
From the drudgeries
Of existence

If we dare
To take right
Actions

Please
Don't complain,
Don't whine and
Don't be cynic

Instead,
Be silent and
Get into the flow of
Positive attitude and
Commitment simply...

Reflection

Let
My essence
Be the destiny
Driven by some
Precious gifts

I know,
Being human,
An unpredictable,
And lack necessary
Moral habits

No wonder,
Why I struggle
Through this
Perpetual
Transition from
Known
To the unknown

I also know,
I yet to be a
Positive force of
Change before
Declaring,

"I've
Arrived at
The center of
All I ought to be..."

In
Perpetuality

It may be a
Flash of my thought
And I still a big wonder,

"Why all seems
A woven web of
Doubts, debates and
Ephemeral
Opinions to chew on"

There has been
A constant thread
Of our Inner Will;
Connecting us
Whatever riddle
That existed once,
Existing today and
Will do so tomorrow

Beyond is
The metaphysical
Unknown where unity,
Eternity and reality
Turns "Nothingness"
And the wheel spins
Again and over again...

Take
Note

Falsity of
Shallow preaching's
Hazardous to the
Intelligent minds

So is the
Pseudo tribal
Claim of different
Divinely names

How long
Awakened beings
Must adhere to such
Illusory state of
Existence

Time to
Wake-up and
Understand, "There
Is always only ONE"

With such
Simple
Common sense,
Is it not time to drop
The stubborn habit
Of sustained ignorance,
At once!

The
Power

Oh this
Awesome
Rational
Mysticism

What a
Shinning
Light between
Right and
Wrong, yes

Between
Certainty and
Possibility alright

Being always
In suspension,
Between
Imperfection and
Perfection to be

Let there be
Neither the
Fear of life nor
Death, but the
Beautiful bliss
All that is to be
Experienced yet...

Revelation

God,
What a
Verily human
Moral spirit,
Simply

God,
No more
Unknown, but
In the human
Thought only

Let us
Free God from
Divided tribal
Claims

Let us
Resuscitate
Him From
The disease of
Ignorance and
Free always...

The Task

While
Riding through
The finite time

Always a
Necessity
Of clarity,
Vision and right
Grasp of the
Journey so planned

Let
Every exploring
Being
Must actualize
The hidden
Meaning of their
Individual soul and
Be awakened in time

Don't forget,
There is always
A necessity of Good
To reach the goal
Before it's too late...

Being &
Reality

In the larger
Perspective of
Reality

I am
Contextual in
My worth and

As am
Measured by
The worldly values
Either right or
Otherwise

That is
The verdict of
My existence
And it is the

Essence of
Misplaced "I"
In these
Spiraling spheres
Of this granted time...

Pivot

If love is
The experience
Of truth

Why
We've been
Writing its
Story half-n-half
Since the very
Beginning

If the
Soul is eternal
Consciousness
Connecting us
With everything in
The universe

Why
Do we need to
Be born in
Human form and
For what purpose

And why be
The fearful and
Ignorant beings
And what for!

Wish

Did you say?
"I will go before
You dear"

I said,
"No, it can't
Be that way ever"

" But why not dear?"

"Cause, I can't
Live without you"

After a pause,
I said, "Why not
We go together to
Eternity at the same
Time, dear"

"I like it. That's
The way
To be forever"

Well, that is the
Glory of all good
Love birds
When
Hitting their
Diamond Jubilee of
Love and grace...

Outcome

In sum
Total of all,
Human is
The embodiment
Of good and evil
At the same time

That reality
Dictates endless
Battle in the mind
Of him/her only

How to
Swing from
The dark to the
Shining light
Been a herculean
Task since
The beginning

Sadly,
He hasn't grasped
Truth of such a
Simple escape even
Today...

Inner
Being

I, a living
Universe of my
Intentions and
I ask,
"Am in sync with
My set mission or
Not"

So I keep
Rolling forward
Through the finite
Time to take care
Of the reason
I am being born

All I've is
Willingness to
Take this chance
Yes, only
My inner spirit
Is the guide and

My moral call
Is to reach the
Shore on time...

The
Aim

While
Standing by the
Edge of life and
Thinking, "How to
Be a moral courage
To spark the noble soul
From this point on"

I see
Dark clouds
Passing through
My sight but they never
End... to clear the view
Of the blue sky

In such a
Cloudy world of
Irrational beliefs

Wish,
We humans
Stand up to clear the
Collective blurs and
Build a reality to
Fit our ideal dream...

Power of
Love

Darling,
In love we
Live and in love
We shall die only

For
There ain't any
In-between to be
So,
I say, "Wake-up
And make it up
For the
Time is so brief"

Let's
Sing the song
When we met for
The first time

Let's
Dance with the
Power of love and
Let us be free from
The crisis on hand...

Glowing
Spirits

Let there
Be light to regain
Solitude, harmony
And good attitude

Let there
Be inner echoes
Asking us to be
A genuine being,
Once again

No need
To interrupt the
Solemn journey by
Being the victims
Of the seven sin

Let
The spiraling
Spheres of rethink,
New imaginations;
Powering the
Mortal beings to
The teasing hills...

The
Magic

In the
Final spike of
The mystical soul
Where
The line between
Life and death is
Defined so well

As a
Consequence,
All bets are off
For the
Continued streams
Of consciousness
Hovers over for
A brief and

Soon after
There is no "I"
On the scene

And that is
The Nano-sec
Reality of life and
Death embracing
At the same time...

That
Is It

**What if
You're not on
The scene any
More**

**Will that
Mean you're
Free to be?**

**What if,
You've missed
The train where
You're the real
Passenger to be!**

**Don't
Blame the cruelty
Of reality any more
Let your
Responsibility
Be the first virtue
Be welcomed from
The very beginning,
That you must...**

World
Prayer

Oh
Almighty who's
The Unity of all
That is

Inspire us
To be good
By reckoning,
"You're One
And One only"

Inform us
That we're One
Big family

Reeducate us
That we're all
Born to look beyond
Our myopic point of
Views

And free
Us from the curse
Of ignorance, violence
And arrogance;
Controlling
Our thick heads..

Being
Alive

As
Lovers,
We've to be the
Directional force;
Delineating,
"What is right and
What is not?"

As
Citizens,
We've to be
The hope and be a
Stubborn courage
To make it all the
Way to be the best

As
Guardians of
Children, it is
Mandatory we
Begin to clean the
Mess on time

If we
Meet all obligations
Soon... would define,
"Who we're and our
Enlightened legacy as well..."

Being
It Is

How do we
Convince human
To believe what is
Best to be

Does he
Ever care to think,
"He's the light that
Shall never fade"

How do we
Convey the message,
"He's the truth of
His own probe"

Does he ever
Care to reckon,
"He's the essence
Of his existence;
Here and beyond"

Does he ever
Care to know,
"He's the destiny
Of his own meaning,
Or not!"

Sacred
Vows

When we
Took the solemn
Vows, at that
Very moment,
We seized the best
What life got
To offer

And,
We became
The inspiring
Freewill's in
Launching the
Great journey
In full earnest

In between
Million challenges,
Hardships and happy
Experiences flew by and

Here
We're at the edge;
Waiting to leap into
Eternity where we shall
Be forever...

Synergy

But,
Sweet Heart,
We're the reality
Of our dreams

No point
In ignoring the
Great stride and
No point in let go
Our best time

Sweet Heart,
Don't be afraid
Just take one bold
Step at a time and
Hold onto promise
At every turn

That is
The power of
Our love at the core
That is
The strength, "Who
We're and what we can
Become through thick
And thin of our time..."

The
Drive

Let it
Drip and drip
Slowly the dreams
We've been holding
For a long

We're the
Continuum of
Grief and joy while
Trying to hold onto
Our love...yes
Into the world of
"Double talks"

Don't ever
Lose your trust
In our love

Don't ever
Doubt the
Consequences of
Being in love

Just keep
Full-faith in our
Mutual strengths
And we shall triumphant
In this challenging journey
Called, "Love..."

On the
Road

As
Rain pours heavier
Than ever before,
Metal wipers
Keeps the windshield
Clear with greater
Mechanical efforts

Sorry,
But the condition
On the road
Doesn't allow me
To brake so well

In such
State of lightening
And thunders,
I keep the car rolling
Through the power of
My love, luck and laughter

Suddenly,
Radio fails and
The music is no more;
Defrosting doesn't work,
As well

In such a
Miserable state, I am
Determined to keep
Going with a full tank
Of my fearless Self...

Revolving Perceptions

A poor man
Observed,
"Though he didn't
Make it to the highest
Point, he understood
The complexities of
Life so well"

A deaf jumped in
And said, "Though
I didn't hear 'em well,
Heard their shallow
Promises, shouts and
Insulting remarks more
Often than I'd ever
Thought"

His wife
Who was mute got
Into the conversation,
"Though I don't speak,
I showed 'em the sign,
To shut-up and move on"

A perfectly
Healthy guy heard 'em
Chat; stopped by to add,
"Gee this existence sucks
As there is no purpose
Left to go on..."

Fun City

What a
Happy exploration
In the city full of
Pleasures

Where
Casinos are
Magnetic attraction
And gambling is the
Biggest adventure

Of course,
Folks aimlessly
Throw coins into
The giant
Machines trying out
Their luck to make
Some free money

Oh the
Awesome nightly
Shows where beautiful
Gals mesmerizing
Millions on the
Glamorous scene

Casinos, bars
And lost visitors
All boozing so
Generously and
Becoming good friends
Atleast for a while...

The
Drama

As I
Keep walking along
The highway of my
Crazy world

I wonder,
What if we're the
Irrational
Consequence or what?

Let's face it,
We're also the
Cause of our progress
And regress both

Is there
A possibility
We've been running
On a wrong track for a
Long or not

Did we
Ever reckon,
"We're the fallen
Victims as we keep
Sustaining the
Forces of ignorance,
Violence and greed..."

New
Reality

Now,
The baby robots
Called, "Xenobots"
Are being born by the
Big numbers from the
Super smart machines

They may be
In infancy today
Who knows what they
Will be tomorrow?

Humanity
Caught into the
Spiraling sphere of
Hypersonic missiles,
Quantum warfares and
Weaponized pathogens
Capable of killing us
By the many millions

The sphere is
Slowly shrinking and
No room left to hide
Yes, there is
No room to save
Humanity from tits
Slow death,

I mean, if we
Ignoring the basic issues
Of survivability at this time...

Lady Swagger

Oh yes,
She's a lady of
Complete beauty

She's quite
Acerbic and very
Independent in her
View as well

She calls
Herself, "I am
The Best always"
And, she gets away
With it for she knows

Men admires
Her tease always,
Even they forget
They're married to
Another beauty too

Oh yes,
The lady is
Smart and knows
So well, "Males are
Her victims and that's
Why she can rule them
As she wishes any time..."

A
Historic
Note

What is the
Meaning of any
Glorified war when
There are destructions
And deaths of millions,
Every time

Sadly,
Historic events
Called,
"Great Wars"
Keep high lightening
Them as
Heroic victories

When
One reads them
There is nothing, but
The thousand pages of
Inhumanity only

Where
Did we go
Wrong in holding
The Moral Equation
That is at the core?

We're Champs

We're the
Winners every
Time

Yes, yes
We're born to
Beat you every
Time

Get ready
And face us,
If you dare

We don't
Give a damn,
"What you think
Of us"

We're here to
Win the game
And that's our
Goal and

Damn right,
We're the winners
Every time when you
Play the game
Against us...

Celebrations

Come let us
Express
Gratitude
To those who
Showed courage
And kindness,
"How to be
Genuine human,
Always"

Come let us
Celebrate
Our truth for
We've endured
Through the rough
Waters of the
Wild Sea

Come let us
Pass on
Good memories
To the children and
Let 'em
In turn do the
Same...

Universal
Norm

Don't you
Run away from
Contradictions,
Chaos and
Confusions

For
They shall
Never leave
Until you triumph
Over them

That's the
Law of Truth for
Those seeking
The adventure

And that's the
Norm for the
Intelligent beings
Who dares to open
The thick steel doors
Called, "The Unknown..."

New
Path

Hello
There my friends,
Just a memento:

"Do you
Know where're
We heading today"

Hello
Good people
Everywhere,
"Do we know,
Why're we so
Silent today"

Hello
Folks, "Why
Don't we be bold
And move the needle
To the right and walk
Along a new path!"

Magnifique Seven

I may be
Still chugging along
This terrain where
Once I walked along
With the
Magnificent Seven

Their love,
Care and courage
Made my life full of
Significance to move
On

In time,
The Seven nobles
Left the road
At different
Points and
Let me
Go on my own

Someday
I will
Rejoin 'em,
But today, I must
Take care of the
Loving ones
While am here...

End Game

Be inspired
And do motivate
Million others

Yes, to take
Responsibility to
Define a unique
Destiny for the
Good

Ensure
That self-renewal
Remains as main
Focus
I mean,
In thoughts, words
And actions at all
Time

Learn to
Keep life in its
Right perspective
So it can be kept
Steady on the track

Time to
Rethink and be
Reborn to enjoy the
True freedom from
Every point on...

Rubicon

Intelligent
Life is the
Harmony with
All that is evolving
From good to ever
Best

Enlightened
Being is the
Moral light to
Grasp of all that is

Historic
Man what
A double-edged
Sword: love & hate,
Right & wrong...being
Victim of the seven sin

Modern
Human too is
Standing at the
Cross-road either
To be a techno-slave
Or a master of his
Destiny before it's
Too late..."

Global
Human

Ain't
Time to move
Forward from
Endless debates to
Action

For challenges
Can be resolved
If we walk together
With a shared purpose

Ain't
Time to become
Good friends and
Begin to seek answers
To our collective
Struggles

For
History will not
Change without our
Awakening;
Powering to act
In the good cause of
The whole...

At
The Core

We're
All that we are
At the core

We're
Everything
That is
Our dream,

And then
Why don't we
Understand,
"Who we're and
What we can
Become?"

That is
Paradox we've
Been ourselves
For a long

That is
The perplex we've
Been throughout
The blessed time...

High Society

Urbane
Hypocrisy
What a far cry
From the simplicity
Of a bucolic beauty

In big cities,
There is an arrogant
Interpretation of
Selfish agenda driven
By the ever hidden
Greed

Their
Glittered world
Is a floating castle
Of sand and

As there is
Not much left to
Renew humanity,
Dignity and honor for
Cities are the creation
Of massive slumps...

Eternal Rhythm

Curiosity and
Creativity ever a
Necessity of
Intelligent beings

That's the first
Step to be a moral
Spark in this
Holistic reality

Birth and death,
Two ends of a single
Thread; stretching
Either long or
Sadly too short and
Such is the nature
Of the battlefield

That's the
Final word in the
Closure of life from
The world of struggle,
All right

And, that's
The beginning of the
Empirical experience
As he moves toward
The meaning of his own
Riddle through time...

Self-Realization

Every
Possibility is a
Passage to wisdom
Either sooner or
Later

Every
Creative Lyric
Too is an
Opening to
New vision either
Sooner or later

That is the
Power of an
Illumined mind
That is the
True faith driven
By reason and
And a nameless
Divine

No point
Rotting with
Shallow views and
The double-talks
For life is one
Precious brief chance...

Inchoate

Did we
Ever realize,
"We're here
For a brief"

Did we
Ever reckon,
"After death,
We're just a
Fading memory"

Knowing
It all, why do
We still remain
Ignorant of our
Own being

That's
The erroneous
Consequence
And we call,
"Us Humans"

Power
To Be

Paradoxically,
We've are
Spontaneously
Awakened Self
Without a thought

If that is
Understood well,
It's the
Turning point,
To accelerate the
Clarification of our
Corrupted thinking
Process

With such a
Miraculous strength,
We got the truth
In our hands without
A long struggle and
Pain

If only,
We are ready
To walk along such a
Daring track!

Attention!

Time to
Walk with a
Moral confidence
To save the soul
Of the troubled
World today

Let
Awakened
Minds
Reverberate the
"Global Spirit"

For
There is an
Urgency to
The situation
We're in today

There is a
Serious need to
Ensure a good
Future to the kids
And we must act...

The Trail

Just
Keep rolling
Along the trail but
With a sense of
Self-confidence and
Goodwill

Nothing to be
Fearful,
Nothing to be
Worried

Just
Keep the
Journey going
With your
Determined will

Let you
Learn,
"How to refine
Your conduct well
While on the trail..."

Janus

He said,
"We're in love"
And she said,
"Not that soon"

"Why such a
Silly answer?"

"Well, you've
Not met my
Parents, yet"

"Aren't you
Your
Own person?"

"Well you've
Always insisted,
You like a girl
Who's well raised
By her parents"

"Touché!"

"Don't you
Touché me"

"Why not?"

"For you're a
Hypocrite and
I can never fall in love
With such a guy even
In my sweetest dream..."

Beware

Day after
Day, folks
Everywhere
Kept churning
Into their mental
Machines

For
They've been
Fed constantly
Through fear and
And uncertainty of
The future

Day after
Day, folks silently
Witnessing;
Waning
Humanity, dignity
And meaning

Yes,
From this
Beautiful world
That is caught into
Violence's, wars and
The dehumanizing
Smart machines...

Ideal
Dream

A well ordered
Society stands
Tall on
The foundation
Of unity built by the
Equal responsibility
And freedom to all

It even
Fosters a great
Harmony
If powered by
The constructive
Character of each
Participating
Citizen

Yes, to build
Such an ideal
Society,
Folks must adapt
To the new reality
Of inclusion and
Tolerance first...

Education
Forever

When
We live in a
Consequential
World

It's
Pertinent,
Not only we
Nourish children
With good values
And right conduct,
But the grow-ups
Must do the same

History
Vividly shows,
"It's the grown-ups
Who've messed-up
The world always"

So let us all
Be educated with
Basic ethics in order
To save human dignity
And a hopeful future
For our kids...

To Be

Let us
Be the fearless
Beings to
Inspire the young
Braves

Let us
Be the rational
Beings
So the young can
Sustain harmony and
Peace

Let us
Be the moral
Beings
So the young
Can stand-tall for
A just cause with
Courage and freewill...

Clarion
Bells

Is it not
Time to bring
A new zeal to the
Otherwise effete
World of ours

Come and
Let us save it
From slipping into the
Hellish realm before
It is too late

Let us band
Together to be
Meaningful in
Regaining the
Fading humanity,
That is us and
Our kids

Is it not
Time to reckon,
"We are the
Masters of our brilliant
Destiny and we must
Remain firm at this point."

My
Case

**While
Being on the
Highway of
Existence**

**"I am"
Just breathing
Expression for a
While**

**Who
Knows what
Issues would be
Challenging
To my inner
Being**

**Let I
Gather all the
Moral strength to
Be free from the
World**

**That is
Lost into the
Myopic
Tribal claims,
Today...**

Twist of
Fate

As I Looked
At my beard,
I realized

It was black
Yesterday while
Being a young man

It turned,
Pepper-gray while
Chugging through the
Middle-age

And suddenly,
It turned silver-white
One day and was I
Surprised!

Life too
Was once blank
And began to turn
Pepper-gray with
Million adventures
And here am today;
Pointing upward with
Every gray in the beard...

Last
Soul

The last Soul
Of humanity goes
Where no other
Has gone before

Yes, that Soul
Shall save wisdom
And transferring it to
The deserving others
In another time

Don't cry and
Don't be jealous
For we had many
Millennia to wise-up
And we didn't

Oh yes,
The last Soul has
Found right hearts,
Minds and receptive
Spirits in the arms
Of the new time

Of course,
To build a world
Of harmony and
Lasting peace,
Far away from
The old times...

Nowhere

While traveling
Along a highway of
Hope
I read the sign,
"Road Ends Soon"

I wondered,
"Why such a sign
In this open terrain
Where there ain't rain;
Only high heat to bear"

I had to
Take a U-turn and
Returned to my distant
Place once again

Again
Another sign came
To my sight,
"Do Not Enter"

Suddenly,
It dawned upon me,
I was a lost human
Into my own
Subjective illusion...

Dear
Heart

Dear Heart
Don't run away
It's just a patch of
Shadow and

That too
Shall fade and
There'll be sunshine
Soon

Dear Heart
Let time heal the
Wounds and

We'll
Return to
The days of love
And laughter soon

Dear Heart,
Don't lose your
Trust for our vows
Been forever

Dear Heart,
Come back and be
The love you're
Always and shall be
The same again...

Our
Time

It's the insane
World we're living
In today
Where
Leaders are being
Busy letting wars after
Wars again

And there is the
Ever challenging
Tribal madness;
Claiming different
Brands while He is
"One" indeed

The mural on
The wall ain't pretty
As we look at it from
The deep moral concern

Come let us
Make sense of
Our collective worth
Through regaining the
Waited rational strength
Before we blow up
The beautiful world...

Aimless

Humanity
At times seems
A marching
Drunken people;

Rolling
Aimlessly
Along a winding
Road and going
Nowhere but to
The gates of chaos
And miscalculations

Sometime, it
Hits an open patch
Of hope and happy
Feelings and

At most others,
Nothing but riots
Killing its dream
And meaning
Each time

Seems
Humanity
Today is ever
Lost between
"What is right and
What is not..."

Sunshine

None other
Than the reality
Beyond conception
Is in my mind
Always

None other
Than be the
Awakened human
I wish to be
Always

No, no
It's not escapism,
But the desire to be
Worthy of my birth,
Only

No, no
It's not quitting
The scene, but am
Waiting to be an
Enlightened spark
Within the grand
Illuminated reality,
Itself...

Retrospective

Thank you
Being my
Other half for
A long time

Thank you
For putting-up
With this guy
With patience,
Love and care

We've
Walked through
Thick and thin of
Each highway and
You're the courage,
Every time

Now, we've
Aged and turned
Frail but our dream
And love remains as
Young when we fell in
Love for the first time...

Think
Future

It's courage
And creative
Thoughts nourishing
Every young to be
The meaning in their
Given time

Let each
See first ray of
Hope and
Be self-confident
And let them be the
Masters of their
Own destiny

Time to
Think of the future
Of young today and
Lend them support
To become better
Humans unlike
Their elders, today

That's the
Only royal road to
Change the world for
Good and that's the
Truth we must welcome,
Every time...

Now,
Is Here

It was
Just another
Day to keep
Rolling with the
Daily struggles

It was
Just yesterday,
We met for the
First time and the
Time flew by so
Soon

Perhaps,
We're in the
Timelessness of
"Nowhere but to
Each other"

What if
Love is the power
Moving us higher
Toward our truth
Or what!

Language

Language
Is a funny world
Where ruler can
Mean a
Measuring stick
Or a person who is
The ruler called,
"King"

There are
Words sounding
The same,
"Deal, kill, skill or
Steal and so on"
But, not many such
For love, hope, moral
Few to mention

It's the
Lingua franca of
Any time that
Stopped us from
Comprehending the
Totality of human
Experience, I guess...

Query

What if
Our cosmic
Birth is an
Evolving essence
Geared
For the good

Why
Then don't
We notice such
An imperceptible
Change through
The dark days of
Our time?

What if
Reality is just
An ever changing
Truth,

Why then we
Pursue the quest
In the name of
What is called,
"The Ultimate!"

Freewill

Either
We're here or
We're never
That's
Where we've
Been since
The beginning
While seeking for
Truth

Either
We remain
Where we've been
In for a long, or
We go
Where there is
A room to awaken
Our moral sense

In such a scenario,
Let us be
Worthy of our
Births and proudly
Declare,
"We're everywhere
And forever..."

Make it, Now

Get
Over the
Edge and get
Over the fear

We say,
"Let's
Go beyond
And bring forth
Some meaning,
"Who we're"

Let's
Keep flying
To the world of
Our common goal

Yes, let's
Get over this
Hang-up and
Destructive habits

And
Bring some
Sanity in order,
In return, please...

Riders

It's the
Soul
That doesn't
Know evil

It's the
Soul
That's always
Pointing to the
Right and

It's the
Hope that's the
Light to the truth
We've been after
For a long

So
Sweet heart,
Let our souls
Journey us from
Here and beyond
Through the power
Of our love...

Beautiful
Words

Why is it,
We all have an
Ideal thoughts to
Be perfect beings
Yet, we fail to meet
The wish

All so sweet
In greeting cards
And birthday wishes
But in reality ...sadly
Never measuring up
To our sincerity at
The core

Imperfect
Beings chasing
To be Perfect
In their thoughts,
Only to report at
This time...

Quintessence

Only
Truth that opens
The door to the
World of Unknown
Is the noble Soul
Simply

Only
Essence that is
Genuine
Self-awareness is
Nothing but all that is

Let
Each soul be,
"An intellectual
Mystical experience"
Always

So where
Morality and
Rationality are the
Real strengths to
Every weakly material
Being...

We're
Reality

Being is a
Moral awakening
To understand all
That is

Being is a
Final step in
Entering the realm
Of truth

It is such
Gathering of
Necessary inner
Strengths
That give him a
New beginning,
Every time

Let it be
Known there is
Something far
Greater in him than
Be an ever struggling
Worm...

On the
Go

Keep
Smiling with
Good thoughts
Always

Keep
Exploring with
Your guts
Always

Know well,
You're the
Defining moment
Of your destiny
Forever

Begin
Your big dream
Today and let
Your genius open-up
All possibilities at once...

New
Dawn

Rejoice folks,
It's a new day
To celebrate our
Collective dream
Today

Of course,
It's a right time
To wake-up our
Global Awareness
Today

Rejoice folks,
It's a new dawn to
March toward,
"Humanity forever"

Rejoice folks,
It's a new vision
To move on toward
A fascinating world

Where we
Shall have Peace and
Moral celebrations,
Always...

Oh the Time!

Swiftly,
But sneakily
Life flew by;
Not leaving enough
Time to fulfill all dreams,
They held in their hearts

They
Thought the world
Was at their feet as
They walked through
The million goals; alas
It was all for a while

Soon children
Entered in their lives
And again it was
All for a while

Suddenly, all their
Ambitions changed
As they ran out of
Precious time and left
The world without
Saying, "Goodbye..."

Sparks

All humans
By nature are
Explorers of the
Unknowns and

Dare
To go over the
Edge and even far
Beyond to know
Their truth

That is
The power of
Their very inner
Being and sadly
Most are not even
Aware of their
Strength

Each is a
An exploding
Creativity in this
Magnifique Universe

And sadly,
Most are not
Caring to know
Their built-in,
Awesome strength...

Dark
Side

This
Creature
Called human
Once a cave dweller

Who through
Generations,
Turned into
A solipsistic
Man of today

All he cares,
Money, fame
And power to be,
Always

Sorry,
There ain't
Modicum
Compassion
Left in him

Only "Money,
Money...money" is
The obsession of his
Craving Self...

Know
'Em well

Modern
Elites, what
An intellectual
Displacements

Do they
Ever know the
Difference between
Right or wrong

Beyond
Phony façade,
Do they ever care
For needy, poor or
The sick

Do them
Ever know, "How
To save goodness
For others too!

Continuum

Always
The present is
Reality that we
Experience with
Awareness,

The past,
It's just a
Faded memory
Since we
Keep repeating the
Same blunders and
Sins...generations
After generation

Well, the future
Remains a wildcard
As ever, but it too
Demands, "Some good
To think about, today..."

Noble
Soul

The soul
In essence is
The moral action
Without a second
Thought

It is always
Touched by the
Rational grasp,
"Who we're and
What we ought
To be"

The soul is
But a stream of
Consciousness
Linking "I" to
The totality of all
That is

The soul,
What an
Embodiment of
The known and the
Unknown holding
My truth as ever...

Criteria

We' must
The meaning to
Proceed with a moral
Mission ahead

God
May be forgiven
When we fail to take
The right action, but
We're to be blamed,
If we don't

Life
What a grand unity,
Only if we treat her
With love and respect
To fulfill our dreams

Time
Indeed is valuable,
If we endeavor, "How
To make the world
Better than before"

Never forget
To inspire the
Young to be bold,
In lifting humanity
In the spirit of Good.

Plain Talk

It's
Necessary
To delete the
Old habits;
Triggering
Deaths and
Destructions

It's
Necessary
We activate
Our common-sense
To survive with
Dignity

If we care
To live in a world
Of good, it's
Necessary we
Open-up our minds

It's
Necessary we
Change our
Attitudes and
Adapt to the
New reality that's
Calling for
Moral action in
Our time...

Rationale

In
The new
Reality of our
Time,
Not God,
But human alone
Is the cause of all
His sufferings

It's not
The Mighty Divine,
But human is the
Writer of history
Full of blunders

Let's
Get off
The blind alley
And

Relearn,
How to be
Good and be
Free from all the
Misdeeds...

The Way

Dare
Pursue
To be in
The state of
Intellectual
Mysticism

And
Let it
Awakened
Our individual
Soul to know
The new path,
"Who we're and
How far to go"

Let it
Reinvigorate
Harmony, hope
And Goodwill
While the
Journey's on...

A
Thought!

**Human
What a
Mysterious entity
As he often keeps
Rolling without
Fully-knowing**

**He
Silently seeks
To walk along the
Highway of
Moral thoughts and
Reason-based insights
Yet he fails to do so**

**Human
Always caught
By the struggles
Of his old stubborn
Pseudo beliefs and
Lacks courage to
Free himself**

**Human,
What a wonderful
Gift who still keeps
Shielding himself behind
The Seven sin...**

Reality Beyond

At times,
It's not the
Explanation
That is
Essential, but
The state of
Thoughtlessness
Carries a deeper
Meaning

I mean,
Look at the
Abstract art
Where reality is
Expressed,
"An awesome
Silence with truth..."

And take a
Gaze at the
Cosmos in the night

Where infinite
Starlight's are
Flashing their
Eternal inspiration
To speed-up
Our search of genuine
Beauty and good...

Love
Magic

Oh the Love,
So sweet, yet
What a big tease
If the dream doesn't
Materialized in time

Love,
What a lasting
Memory that never
Leaves the heart

Love
What a
Double-edged
Sword that cuts
Both ways and the
Wound takes long
To heal

Even while
Walking through
Such a
Serrated ridge,

Love
What an imminent
Force between two
Waiting hearts who
Can't wait to be one...

Long Walk

I know,
I've been aimlessly
Spinning into this big
Sphere of the unknown
To go from here to
Over there

And that's the
Way it has been
Since beginning and
That I can't ignore
While am on the road

Time I
Get ready to adapt
To the new reality at
Every turning point

For I know the
Road has been
Winding all the way
To the final exist

Now I must
Open-up a new trail
To reach from here to
Over there on my own
Borrowed time...

Paradox

In spite being
Born with a gift of
Reason and moral
Sense

Why is he
Suffering from
Anxiety and fear
Every now and then

Being,
Yes the modern
Human indeed came
To the world to know,
"What is it all about?"

Why is he
Slumbering while
Best dream is fading,
Away from his
Common sense

Being, oh yes
The intelligent one,
Why hasn't he
Awakened to the
Moral call of his time...

Big
Picture

Let us
Live where humans
Are free and equal
In their existence

Let it
Be the world
Where each is
Respected as precious
Living unit of humanity

Let it
Be the new attitude
To sustain harmony,
Peace and dignity of
All

Be sure
Each carries out
Responsibility before
Demanding individual
Rights and that must
Be the first moral step...

Our
Story

Where
Every human
Grows, changes and
Becomes something
Either/or

It is the
Continued drama
Of the inner motives
Triggering either
Good or otherwise

Again,
All that is, seems
Subjective judgment
Of still not-so fully
Developed human
Mind

No wonder,
Why the world
Is in the spin-tail
Of million negative
Forces; generated by
Humans, essentially!

Mission
Assigned

All
Has been
For now and
For a
While only

Why then
Waste life when
It's so brief

Ain't
Time
To wake-up
From the long
Slumber, now

No point
In dwelling with
Pseudo-narratives
And trivialities

Ain't
Time to stand-up
And be counted for
Something larger than
Life to be!

Be Alert

What sort of
Goal one has in
The mind,
Defines the
Mission of life
Over a time

What
One desires and
Endeavors with a
Sincerity to succeed

He shall be the
Master sculptor of
His dreams come
True while riding
Through his time

Though
He got all the
Possibilities,
Yet no
Such guarantees
Where uncertainty
Rules the world...

Sweet
Slumber

In this grand
Spiraling sphere of
Subjectivity, chaos
And contradictions

Still
Human illumines,
His perpetually
Expanding
Noble Spirit indeed

It is only
Through creative
Thoughts in art, music
And deep silence;
Begins to reckon the
Mystical truth for
The first time

Human
Still a perpetually
Exploding creativity;
Looking for
His forgotten meaning!

Being
As Is

Being
In essence
Is a continuum

Only
Then he shall
Reckon his moral
Self in full

Being alone
Interprets the
World experience
He's in

Being is the
Constant flow of
Consciousness;
Generation to another
Defining it as his
Truth

Being,
What a mystical
Riddle yet to be known
In toto either without
A doubt or a debate...

The
Direction

Where the
Spirit flow, defines
The glow of a journey
To be

In such
A bold adventure,
The enlightened soul
Is the difference
Maker

While
All is rolling
Along a narrow
Strip of the known
And the unknown

And all is a
Constant growth
And change: from
Imperfection
To perfection and.
From darkness to Light

Let the
Spiraling desires,
Ambitions and wants
Be refined at every
Turning point...

Disintegration

Million
Scattered
Virtues
Falling off the
Reality and
No one's paying
Attention to 'em

In such a
Heartless
Dominion of
No concern, how
Long humanity
Can go on?

Nothing
Seems certain
As it appears and
Nothing seems to
Be Truth as it is
Being preached

Let
Every human
Understand well,
"Nothing is worth
Unless he is an
Enlightened Being...

Holistic
Reality

Intelligent
Soul
Never defined
By the set laws
And rules of man

Yes, it's
The
Inner Spirit
That is the
Only link of
Inspiration

Between
Temporal and
The
Eternal whatever
It may!

No its
Neither a mirage
Nor a fantasy just
An elegant insight
To know the truth for
One Self...

Being &
Destiny

Go
Where your
Will take you to
Be the meaning

I mean,
Go where your
Mission is waiting
In the wing already

Go
Where the
Moral Self
Rides you
To the waiting
Dream

I mean,
Know well,
"You've only one
Life to live and
That is just a brief,
Experience only..."

Confession

Divine
Is not dead, but
Human may

See the
World as is
Where nothing
But the killer
Storms are

Hitting every
Corner of the
Stirred-up
Humans, today

Truth
Never to be
Doubted, but the
Human mind must

Again,
Life is not
Imperfect, but
The stubborn
Ignorant humans
Is the suspect always...

Modern
Elites

That thin
Veil of an
Idealogy geared to
Control the masses,
Of course through
Sweet shibboleths and
Phony smiles always

It's the
Age old game of
The elites whose
Obsessed to be
In power for
Personal gains,
Simply

Globalization
What a latent
Colonialism while
Betraying the quality
Of humanity to the
Billions

Oh, they love to
Control thoughts,
To make more profits
Without accountability,
In return as always...

Invitation

Dear Heart
Come and
Dance with
Me tonight

Don't
Sit alone while
Good times is
Rolling by

Dear Heart
But why your
Pride is stopping
You to be with
Me tonight

I say,
"Seize the
Moment" and be
Happy to dance with
This guy

Damn right,
Who's
Waiting since
The party begun
Tonight...

The
Spiral

**Nature
What a manifested
Myriad forms of
Beauty & Truth**

**Life too
What a spinning
Cycle of birth and
Death**

**All is being
Born to be something
Greater than what it was**

**All is struggling
And suffering and
Yet to be healed in time**

**All seems
Nothing but the revolving
Riddles; teasing the rational
Mind always...**

Missing
Equation

When respect
For law and order
Is maintained well,
Any society shall
Have a better chance
To be stable and safe

When
Selfless guardians
Are at the helm,
"There is a greater
Enhanced moral
Awareness and the
Precious Peace shall
Prevail for a long"

Where
A society achieves
Greater social maturity,
"There is harmony, hope
And human dignity "and

The young braves
Would say, "Thank you
For leaving a world of
Happy place for us..."

Being & Meaning

To be
Aware means
Knowing the inner
Strengths: morality,
Reason and esthetics
Of all there is

To be
Self-realized
Means birth be
Redeemed via exercise
Of good thoughts, words
And deeds

To be
Enlightened means
To posses calm and
Be alert of the Self
And the world around,
At all time

To be the truth
In human form
Means to
Understand how
To enhance the
Very dignity of
Humanity always...

Be
Tough

Nothing is
Impossible but the
Doubtful human is

Nothing is
So steep to climb
But the attitude is

Never
Stand still and
Feel sorry for the
Self

Just keep
Going with a
Doubly determined
Will what may
Be the consequence

Life always
Demands a stiff jolt,
So be bold to be
The creator of your
Possibilities and dare
To succeed what may
The consequence...

In Love

Hey
Girl of my
Dream
Ain't time to
Fall in love, again

Come and see,
How love is
So silently painting
Our new adventure
To be

Hey dear
Heart come and
Be the rider of
Life together with
Me

Come and
Fly with me to
The world of our
Sweet dreams

Dear Heart,
This is our moment
To seize
Yes, that is
The reality where
We must be...

The
Nameless

Complete
Godly ignorance
Driven by the seven
Sin sets the world on
Fire now and then

I mean,
It hurts
Humanity
To the core
As violence's,
Wars and deaths;
Keep on abusing His
Good Name

Belief injected
With poison is called,
"Sheer insanity" and
Can't ever be a
Godly gift

There is
Only One,
And time
To be awakened
To this simple truth
And be the better
Humans for a change...

Being &
Magic

Human
Connectivity is a
Life line that keeps
His meaning evolving
Forever

Human,
A complete contextual
Being who is cognitively,
Emotively and socially
Dependable to know,
"Who He Is"

In such
A closely webbed
Reality,
Wonder what is the
Value of his individual
Freedom and solipsistic
Whims!

Human
Connectivity not
Just in the finite
Spiraling sphere, but
Continuing beyond
All the way
To eternity may be...

Common Sense

The more
We focus via
Introspection,
More
We begin to
Understand the
Meaning of reality,
In time

The more
We give than
Take while on
The pilgrimage
Of our truth;
We're the winners,
In any case

That is
How love,
Courage and life
Take us to the
Happy place always

That is the
Simple and elegant
Truth to be grasped
By the ignorant us,
Yet!

Final
Word

Did we
Ever reckon,
"We're the sovereign
Born to attain the
Noble mission only"

Beyond it,
All seems nothing
But flashes of falsity,
Revenge and greed;
Destroying the truth
Of being real human

Human
Absolutely is the
Expression of
His own moral
Justification and

That is
To ensure a
World of unity, liberty
And responsibility as his
Best experience...

The
Essence

Life
Asks to make right
Choices to be happy
And fulfill the waiting
Goal, if possible

That's why,
Essential to be a
Person of disciplined
Mind with a strong
Will to be awakened
On time

Life
Demands let
Every being be the
Foremost consideration

For
He alone can be
The master of his own
Destiny and that is
The Truth he mustn't
Ever forget...

Truth

As time
Keeps on rolling
Everything keeps
Changing along

So do
Opinions, values
And the notions of
The Divine too

As human
Moves on from
Past to the
Present and
Thinks of future

He too
Becomes a
Different person
Time after time

As riddles,
Puzzles and
Enigmas are
Always there to
Keep challenging
His evolving mind...

Guiding
Light

It is
Best experience
Of 'Self-realization'
That leads the way to
The highest joy

It is the
Guiding light
Showing the path
Through the dark,
Now and then

Know well,
It is actualization
Of moral mind,
When human
Hits the road to
Becoming Divine

Let him keep
Rolling toward a
Beautiful state of
Bliss and be the
Pure Freewill...what
He has been always...

Perceptivity

Control of
Individual
Attitude and
Desires is essential
In evolving as a
Total awakened
Being

Control of the
Seven sin is a
Necessity to be a
Moral being ever

That's
Where
The attention be
During the
Formative years

Control of
Daily conduct is a
Must for it projects
Ones image to the
World

Control of
Opinions and views
Be weighed well to
Save humanity at
Each step of the way...

Façade

The whole
Universe may not be
Created, at one time,
But each bubble was

Each bubble,
In turn had its own
Creation, sustainment,
Destruction and rebirth,
Time and again

In this context,
Let it be clear,
God was never
Before only human
Brought the notion
Out of his fear and
Anxiety of the unknown

Well a few
Shrewed men seized
The opp; turning it into
A man-made belief enterprise

But they failed
To change human nature
Ever and the quest for
Harmony, Peace and
Meaning of the lost
A human is still on...

Being &
Truth

Truth
May be called,
Anything since
It may be
Unknown to the
Three-pound
Thinking machine

Let it
Be God, theory of
Everything or
Whatever pops-up in
Human thought

What if
Truth may
Be the conundrum
Of the human mind,
Forever

And its quest
Just the intellectual
Ride to the realm called,
"Nothingness" or
What!

Let
Freedom
Ring

**Do we
Ever know,
"Being alone is a
Spontaneous insight
That is far greater in
Possibilities than
He thinks"**

**Did we
Ever reckon,
"Intelligent being
Needs no "Dos and
Don'ts" from the
Corrupt preachers
Peddling a
Myopic belief**

**Let modern
Humans be
Progressive
Let them have
Freedom to think
And act for the
Good of the whole...**

We Dare

A notion is
Whatever
The reason
Of understanding,
When we think

In the
Empirical reality,
It carries quite a
Weight and mustn't
Be ignored

It's all about
Connecting the
Constant stream of
Sensory-impressions

As a consequence,
Humans keep spinning
Into the sphere of doubts,
Debates and in conclusions
And that we know so well

Let's dare
Go beyond in the realm
Of "Silence" and experience
The very meaningful noble
Soul within...

Be
Somebody

Our
Task is to be
The illumined mind
And lift humanity
Far away from the
Prevailing dark

That is
How we must
Begin the journey
On a right track

That is
How we become
Friends and not foes
For a common cause

In turn,
Let's declared
With one voice,

"We are born
To be worthy of
Our existence...yes by
Changing the troubled
World into Good."

Fearless
Specks

We're
But tiny specks
In this mighty
Universe

Though
We're petite in
Many respects,
We're
Also the sparks that
Can think far and
Beyond

We're
Here to clarify
The complexities
Of the world we're
Dwelling in

We're
Everything in this
Vast Universe and
We shall prevail
Forever...

Fighters

Come
And let's
Begin the walk
Toward an
Enlightened future
From this point on

Yes, we
Can make it all
The way to the
Final point

For we're the
Rational thoughts
And we can walk
Along a right path

We're
Driven by hope,
Harmony and
Freewill always

Come, let us
Be determined
Souls to reach the
Final goal,

No matter,
What may be the
Consequence at the
End...

A Note

If a belief
Breeds ignorance,
Myth and superstition,
Trash it as soon you
Must

If a guardian
Keeps triggering
Violence's and wars,
Now and then
Drop him as soon as
You must

To be
An enlightened
Being, learn how
To rid off the negative
Forces from the mind

Only
Then a person got
Better chance to save
The meaning of his
Genuine humanity
In time...

Future,
Here

It is
Important to
Remember:

Let
Every being
Born today
Shall have a
Greater chance
To be the hero
Of tomorrow

Let him
Stand tall and be
A shining hope
To the whole

Let him
Lift his moral
Strength to the
Highest point and

Let him
Inspired to be
The good for the
First time...

Nova
Human

God is an
Exclusive thought
Of the human only
In this universe

It's an
Abstraction loaded
With riddles, prayers
And fear of the
Unknown consequence

Let human
Grasp, "He's the
Ultimate reality;
Defining his own
Ethics, choices and
Waiting legacy indeed"

Why then be in
A constant obsession
Of this abstruse Divine
With so much ignorance!

Journey, "Half-way"

Perceptuality
Not enough to lead
A life of total meaning
For existence is
Always a perennial
Uncertainty

Existence
Seems fired-up by the
Million memories,
Dreams and whims of
The human mind only

Of course,
Human keeps
Recycling through
The Spiraling Sphere,
Time and time again,
But progress remains
At snail speed

Well,
The unwritten
Thoughts still
Steady and mute, and
The journey only
Half-way through...

JAGDISH J. BHATT, PhD
Brings 45 years of academic experience
including a post- doctorate research scientist
at Stanford University, CA. He holds an
impressive authorship of 50 books.

Made in the USA
Columbia, SC
11 September 2022

66933785R00088